THIS

JOURNAL

BELONGS TO

ONE LINE A DAY

A FIVE-YEAR MEMORY BOOK

CHRONICLE BOOKS
SAN FRANCISCO

Dana Tanamachi is a New York City–based illustrator, artist, and founder of her boutique design studio, Tanamachi Studio. She is known for intricate linework inspired by Art Nouveau and Japanese patterns, and her typography and illustration can be seen on everything from postage stamps to immersive murals.

ISBN 978-1-7972-3120-4

Manufactured in China.

MIX
Paper | Supporting responsible forestry
FSC
www.fsc.org   FSC™ C136333

Design by Dana Tanamachi.

10 9 8 7 6 5 4 3 2 1

Chronicle Books LLC
680 Second Street
San Francisco, California 94107
www.chroniclebooks.com

A CONDENSED,
COMPARATIVE
RECORD FOR
FIVE YEARS, FOR
RECORDING EVENTS
MOST WORTHY OF
REMEMBRANCE.

HOW TO USE THIS BOOK

To begin, turn to today's calendar date and fill
in the year at the top of the page's first entry.
Here, you can add your thoughts on the present
day's events. On the next day, turn the page and fill
in the year accordingly. Do likewise throughout
the year. When the year has ended, start the next
year in the second entry space on the page,
and so on through the remaining years.

20 _____ _____
_____
_____
_____
_____

20 _____ _____
_____
_____
_____
_____

20 _____ _____
_____
_____
_____
_____

20 _____ _____
_____
_____
_____
_____

20 _____ _____
_____
_____
_____
_____

20 ___

20 ___

20 ___

20 ___

20 ___

· JANUARY 3 ·

20___ _____

20___ _____

20___ _____

20___ _____

20___ _____

20 ___ _____

20 ___ _____

20 ___ _____

20 ___ _____

20 ___ _____

20 ___ _____
_____
_____
_____
_____

20 ___ _____
_____
_____
_____
_____

20 ___ _____
_____
_____
_____
_____

20 ___ _____
_____
_____
_____
_____

20 ___ _____
_____
_____
_____
_____

20 _____ _____

20 _____ _____

20 _____ _____

20 _____ _____

20 _____ _____

20 ___ _____

20 ___ _____

20 ___ _____

20 ___ _____

20 ___ _____

20 _____ _____

_____

_____

_____

_____

20 _____ _____

_____

_____

_____

_____

20 _____ _____

_____

_____

_____

_____

20 _____ _____

_____

_____

_____

_____

20 _____ _____

_____

_____

_____

_____

20___ _____

20___ _____

20___ _____

20___ _____

20___ _____

20 ___

20 ___

20 ___

20 ___

20 ___

20 ___ _____

20 ___ _____

20 ___ _____

20 ___ _____

20 ___ _____

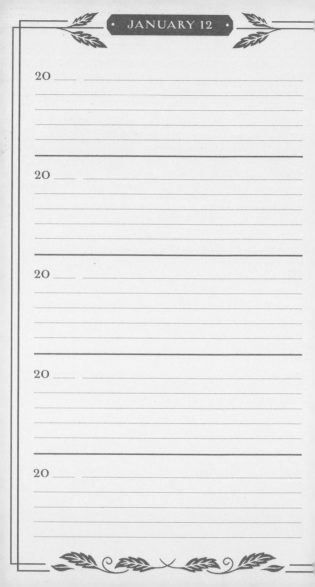

JANUARY 12

20 _____ _____

20 _____ _____

20 _____ _____

20 _____ _____

20 _____ _____

JANUARY 13

20 ___ _____

20 ___ _____

20 ___ _____

20 ___ _____

20 ___ _____

20 _____ _____
_____
_____
_____
_____

20 _____ _____
_____
_____
_____
_____

20 _____ _____
_____
_____
_____
_____

20 _____ _____
_____
_____
_____
_____

20 _____ _____
_____
_____
_____
_____

20 _____ _____

_____

_____

_____

_____

20 _____ _____

_____

_____

_____

_____

20 _____ _____

_____

_____

_____

_____

20 _____ _____

_____

_____

_____

_____

20 _____ _____

_____

_____

_____

_____

20 __ _____

20 __ _____

20 __ _____

20 __ _____

20 __ _____

20 ___ _____
_____
_____
_____
_____

20 ___ _____
_____
_____
_____
_____

20 ___ _____
_____
_____
_____
_____

20 ___ _____
_____
_____
_____
_____

20 ___ _____
_____
_____
_____
_____

· JANUARY 18 ·

20 ___ _____

20 ___ _____

20 ___ _____

20 ___ _____

20 ___ _____

20 _____ _____
_____
_____
_____
_____

20 _____ _____
_____
_____
_____
_____

20 _____ _____
_____
_____
_____
_____

20 _____ _____
_____
_____
_____
_____

20 _____ _____
_____
_____
_____
_____

20 ___ _____
_____
_____
_____
_____

20 ___ _____
_____
_____
_____
_____

20 ___ _____
_____
_____
_____
_____

20 ___ _____
_____
_____
_____
_____

20 ___ _____
_____
_____
_____
_____

20 _____

20 _____

20 _____

20 _____

20 _____

20 ___ _____

20 ___ _____

20 ___ _____

20 ___ _____

20 ___ _____

20 _____ _____

20 _____ _____

20 _____ _____

20 _____ _____

20 _____ _____

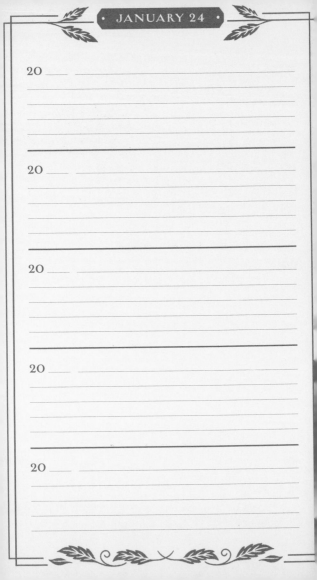

JANUARY 24

20 ___ _____

20 ___ _____

20 ___ _____

20 ___ _____

20 ___ _____

· JANUARY 25 ·

20 _____ _____

20 _____ _____

20 _____ _____

20 _____ _____

20 _____ _____

20 ___ _____

20 ___ _____

20 ___ _____

20 ___ _____

20 ___ _____

20 ___ _____

_____

_____

_____

_____

20 ___ _____

_____

_____

_____

_____

20 ___ _____

_____

_____

_____

_____

20 ___ _____

_____

_____

_____

_____

20 ___ _____

_____

_____

_____

_____

20 ___ _____

20 ___ _____

20 ___ _____

20 ___ _____

20 ___ _____

20____ _____
_____
_____
_____
_____

20____ _____
_____
_____
_____
_____

20____ _____
_____
_____
_____
_____

20____ _____
_____
_____
_____
_____

20____ _____
_____
_____
_____
_____

20 _____ _____

20 _____ _____

20 _____ _____

20 _____ _____

20 _____ _____

20 ___ _____
_____
_____
_____
_____

20 ___ _____
_____
_____
_____
_____

20 ___ _____
_____
_____
_____
_____

20 ___ _____
_____
_____
_____
_____

20 ___ _____
_____
_____
_____
_____

FEBRUARY 1

20 _____ _____
_____
_____
_____
_____

20 _____ _____
_____
_____
_____
_____

20 _____ _____
_____
_____
_____
_____

20 _____ _____
_____
_____
_____
_____

20 _____ _____
_____
_____
_____
_____

20 ___ _____

_____

_____

_____

20 ___ _____

_____

_____

_____

20 ___ _____

_____

_____

_____

20 ___ _____

_____

_____

_____

20 ___ _____

_____

_____

_____

20____ _____

_____

_____

_____

_____

20____ _____

_____

_____

_____

_____

20____ _____

_____

_____

_____

_____

20____ _____

_____

_____

_____

_____

20____ _____

_____

_____

_____

_____

20 ___

20 ___

20 ___

20 ___

20 ___

20 _____

20 _____

20 _____

20 _____

20 _____

20 ___

20 ___

20 ___

20 ___

20 ___

20 ___ _____

_____

_____

_____

_____

20 ___ _____

_____

_____

_____

_____

20 ___ _____

_____

_____

_____

_____

20 ___ _____

_____

_____

_____

_____

20 ___ _____

_____

_____

_____

_____

20 ___ _____

20 ___ _____

20 ___ _____

20 ___ _____

20 ___ _____

20 ___ _____

20 ___ _____

20 ___ _____

20 ___ _____

20 ___ _____

20 ___

20 ___

20 ___

20 ___

20 ___

FEBRUARY 11

20 ___ _____

_____

_____

_____

_____

20 ___ _____

_____

_____

_____

_____

20 ___ _____

_____

_____

_____

_____

20 ___ _____

_____

_____

_____

_____

20 ___ _____

_____

_____

_____

_____

20 ___ _____

20 ___ _____

20 ___ _____

20 ___ _____

20 ___ _____

20 ___ _____
_____
_____
_____
_____
_____

20 ___ _____
_____
_____
_____
_____
_____

20 ___ _____
_____
_____
_____
_____
_____

20 ___ _____
_____
_____
_____
_____
_____

20 ___ _____
_____
_____
_____
_____

· FEBRUARY 14 ·

20 _____

20 _____

20 _____

20 _____

20 _____

20 ___ _____

20 ___ _____

20 ___ _____

20 ___ _____

20 ___ _____

20 __ _____
_____
_____
_____
_____
_____

20 __ _____
_____
_____
_____
_____
_____

20 __ _____
_____
_____
_____
_____
_____

20 __ _____
_____
_____
_____
_____
_____

20 __ _____
_____
_____
_____
_____
_____

20 ___ _____

20 ___ _____

20 ___ _____

20 ___ _____

20 ___ _____

20 ___ _____
_____
_____
_____
_____

20 ___ _____
_____
_____
_____
_____

20 ___ _____
_____
_____
_____
_____

20 ___ _____
_____
_____
_____
_____

20 ___ _____
_____
_____
_____
_____

20 ___ _____

20 ___ _____

20 ___ _____

20 ___ _____

20 ___ _____

20 ____ _____

_____

_____

_____

_____

20 ____ _____

_____

_____

_____

_____

20 ____ _____

_____

_____

_____

_____

20 ____ _____

_____

_____

_____

_____

20 ____ _____

_____

_____

_____

_____

FEBRUARY 21

20 _____ _____
_____
_____
_____
_____

20 _____ _____
_____
_____
_____
_____

20 _____ _____
_____
_____
_____
_____

20 _____ _____
_____
_____
_____
_____

20 _____ _____
_____
_____
_____
_____

FEBRUARY 22

20 ___ _____
_____
_____
_____
_____

20 ___ _____
_____
_____
_____
_____

20 ___ _____
_____
_____
_____
_____

20 ___ _____
_____
_____
_____
_____

20 ___ _____
_____
_____
_____
_____

20 ___ _____

20 ___ _____

20 ___ _____

20 ___ _____

20 ___ _____

20 ___ _____

_____

_____

_____

_____

20 ___ _____

_____

_____

_____

_____

20 ___ _____

_____

_____

_____

_____

20 ___ _____

_____

_____

_____

_____

20 ___ _____

_____

_____

_____

_____

20 _____ _____

20 _____ _____

20 _____ _____

20 _____ _____

20 _____ _____

20 ___ _____

20 ___ _____

20 ___ _____

20 ___ _____

20 ___ _____

20 ___ _____

20 ___ _____

20 ___ _____

20 ___ _____

20 ___ _____

20 _____ _____
_____
_____
_____
_____

20 _____ _____
_____
_____
_____
_____

20 _____ _____
_____
_____
_____
_____

20 _____ _____
_____
_____
_____
_____

20 _____ _____
_____
_____
_____
_____

20 _____ _____

_____

_____

_____

_____

20 _____ _____

_____

_____

_____

_____

20 _____ _____

_____

_____

_____

_____

20 _____ _____

_____

_____

_____

_____

20 _____ _____

_____

_____

_____

_____

20 ___ _____

_____

_____

_____

_____

20 ___ _____

_____

_____

_____

_____

20 ___ _____

_____

_____

_____

_____

20 ___ _____

_____

_____

_____

_____

20 ___ _____

_____

_____

_____

_____

20 _____ _____

_____

_____

_____

_____

20 _____ _____

_____

_____

_____

_____

20 _____ _____

_____

_____

_____

_____

20 _____ _____

_____

_____

_____

_____

20 _____ _____

_____

_____

_____

_____

20 ___ _____

_____

_____

_____

_____

20 ___ _____

_____

_____

_____

_____

20 ___ _____

_____

_____

_____

_____

20 ___ _____

_____

_____

_____

_____

20 ___ _____

_____

_____

_____

_____

20 _____ _____

_____

_____

_____

_____

20 _____ _____

_____

_____

_____

_____

20 _____ _____

_____

_____

_____

_____

20 _____ _____

_____

_____

_____

_____

20 _____ _____

_____

_____

_____

_____

MARCH 5

20 ___

20 ___

20 ___

20 ___

20 ___

20 __ _____
_____
_____
_____
_____
_____

20 __ _____
_____
_____
_____
_____
_____

20 __ _____
_____
_____
_____
_____
_____

20 __ _____
_____
_____
_____
_____
_____

20 __ _____
_____
_____
_____
_____
_____

20 ___ _____

20 ___ _____

20 ___ _____

20 ___ _____

20 ___ _____

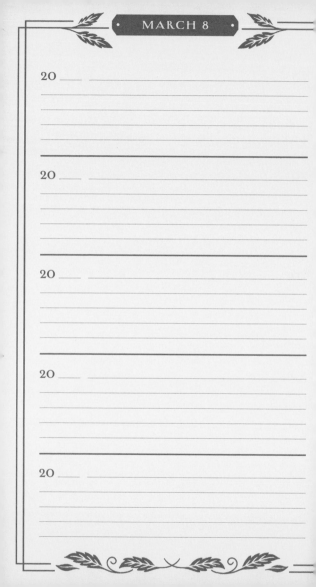

MARCH 8

20 ___ _____

_____

_____

_____

_____

_____

20 ___ _____

_____

_____

_____

_____

_____

20 ___ _____

_____

_____

_____

_____

_____

20 ___ _____

_____

_____

_____

_____

_____

20 ___ _____

_____

_____

_____

_____

_____

MARCH 9

20___ _____

20___ _____

20___ _____

20___ _____

20___ _____

MARCH 10

20___ _____

20___ _____

20___ _____

20___ _____

20___ _____

20 _____ _____
_____
_____
_____
_____

20 _____ _____
_____
_____
_____
_____

20 _____ _____
_____
_____
_____
_____

20 _____ _____
_____
_____
_____
_____

20 _____ _____
_____
_____
_____
_____

MARCH 12

20 _____ _____

20 _____ _____

20 _____ _____

20 _____ _____

20 _____ _____

MARCH 13

20___ _____

20___ _____

20___ _____

20___ _____

20___ _____

20 ___ _____

20 ___ _____

20 ___ _____

20 ___ _____

20 ___ _____

20 ___ _____

_____

_____

_____

_____

20 ___ _____

_____

_____

_____

_____

20 ___ _____

_____

_____

_____

_____

20 ___ _____

_____

_____

_____

_____

20 ___ _____

_____

_____

_____

_____

MARCH 16

20 ___ _____

_____

_____

_____

_____

20 ___ _____

_____

_____

_____

_____

20 ___ _____

_____

_____

_____

_____

20 ___ _____

_____

_____

_____

_____

20 ___ _____

_____

_____

_____

_____

20 _____ _____

20 _____ _____

20 _____ _____

20 _____ _____

20 _____ _____

20 ___ _____

20 ___ _____

20 ___ _____

20 ___ _____

20 ___ _____

20 _____ _____

20 _____ _____

20 _____ _____

20 _____ _____

20 _____ _____

20 ___ _____

20 ___ _____

20 ___ _____

20 ___ _____

20 ___ _____

20 ___ _____
_____
_____
_____
_____

20 ___ _____
_____
_____
_____
_____

20 ___ _____
_____
_____
_____
_____

20 ___ _____
_____
_____
_____
_____

20 ___ _____
_____
_____
_____
_____

MARCH 22

20___ _____

_____

_____

_____

_____

20___ _____

_____

_____

_____

_____

20___ _____

_____

_____

_____

_____

20___ _____

_____

_____

_____

_____

20___ _____

_____

_____

_____

_____

20 ___ _____

20 ___ _____

20 ___ _____

20 ___ _____

20 ___ _____

20 ___ _____

20 ___ _____

20 ___ _____

20 ___ _____

20 ___ _____

20 _____

20 _____

20 _____

20 _____

20 _____

20 ___ _____

20 ___ _____

20 ___ _____

20 ___ _____

20 ___ _____

MARCH 27

20 _____ _____
_____
_____
_____
_____

20 _____ _____
_____
_____
_____
_____

20 _____ _____
_____
_____
_____
_____

20 _____ _____
_____
_____
_____
_____

20 _____ _____
_____
_____
_____
_____

MARCH 28

20 ___ _____

20 ___ _____

20 ___ _____

20 ___ _____

20 ___ _____

20 ___ _____
_____
_____
_____
_____
_____

20 ___ _____
_____
_____
_____
_____
_____

20 ___ _____
_____
_____
_____
_____
_____

20 ___ _____
_____
_____
_____
_____
_____

20 ___ _____
_____
_____
_____
_____
_____

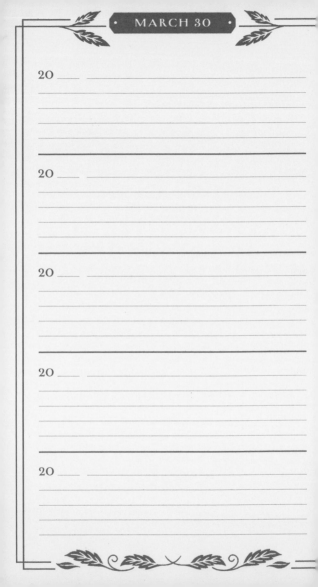

MARCH 30

20___

20___

20___

20___

20___

· MARCH 31 ·

20____ _____

20____ _____

20____ _____

20____ _____

20____ _____

20 ___ _____

20 ___ _____

20 ___ _____

20 ___ _____

20 ___ _____

APRIL 2

20 _____ _____

20 _____ _____

20 _____ _____

20 _____ _____

20 _____ _____

20 _____ _____
_____
_____
_____
_____

20 _____ _____
_____
_____
_____
_____

20 _____ _____
_____
_____
_____
_____

20 _____ _____
_____
_____
_____
_____

20 _____ _____
_____
_____
_____
_____

APRIL 4

20 _____ _____

20 _____ _____

20 _____ _____

20 _____ _____

20 _____ _____

APRIL 5

20 _____ _____

_____

_____

_____

_____

20 _____ _____

_____

_____

_____

_____

20 _____ _____

_____

_____

_____

_____

20 _____ _____

_____

_____

_____

_____

20 _____ _____

_____

_____

_____

_____

20 _____ _____

20 _____ _____

20 _____ _____

20 _____ _____

20 _____ _____

20 ___ _____

_____

_____

_____

_____

20 ___ _____

_____

_____

_____

_____

20 ___ _____

_____

_____

_____

_____

20 ___ _____

_____

_____

_____

_____

20 ___ _____

_____

_____

_____

_____

APRIL 8

20 ___ _____

20 ___ _____

20 ___ _____

20 ___ _____

20 ___ _____

20 ___ _____

_____

_____

_____

_____

20 ___ _____

_____

_____

_____

20 ___ _____

_____

_____

_____

_____

20 ___ _____

_____

_____

_____

20 ___ _____

_____

_____

_____

_____

20 ___ _____
_____
_____
_____
_____
_____

20 ___ _____
_____
_____
_____
_____
_____

20 ___ _____
_____
_____
_____
_____
_____

20 ___ _____
_____
_____
_____
_____
_____

20 ___ _____
_____
_____
_____
_____

20 ___ _____
_____
_____
_____
_____

20 ___ _____
_____
_____
_____
_____

20 ___ _____
_____
_____
_____
_____

20 ___ _____
_____
_____
_____
_____

20 ___ _____
_____
_____
_____
_____

20 ___ _____

_____

_____

_____

_____

20 ___ _____

_____

_____

_____

_____

20 ___ _____

_____

_____

_____

_____

20 ___ _____

_____

_____

_____

_____

20 ___ _____

_____

_____

_____

_____

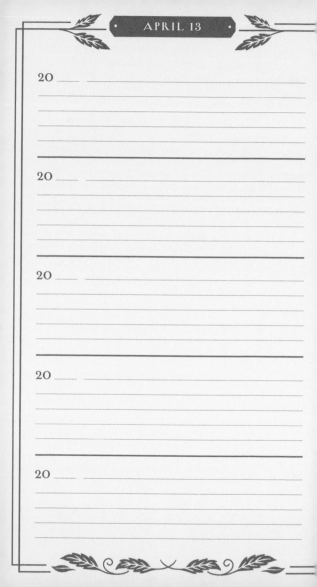

APRIL 13

20 ___ _____

20 ___ _____

20 ___ _____

20 ___ _____

20 ___ _____

20 ___ _____

20 ___ _____

20 ___ _____

20 ___ _____

20 ___ _____

20 ___ _____
_____
_____
_____
_____

20 ___ _____
_____
_____
_____
_____

20 ___ _____
_____
_____
_____
_____

20 ___ _____
_____
_____
_____
_____

20 ___ _____
_____
_____
_____
_____

20 _____ _____
_____
_____
_____
_____

20 _____ _____
_____
_____
_____
_____

20 _____ _____
_____
_____
_____
_____

20 _____ _____
_____
_____
_____
_____

20 _____ _____
_____
_____
_____
_____

APRIL 17

20___ _____

20___ _____

20___ _____

20___ _____

20___ _____

20 ___ _____
_____
_____
_____
_____

20 ___ _____
_____
_____
_____
_____

20 ___ _____
_____
_____
_____
_____

20 ___ _____
_____
_____
_____
_____

20 ___ _____
_____
_____
_____
_____

20____ _____
_____
_____
_____
_____

20____ _____
_____
_____
_____
_____

20____ _____
_____
_____
_____
_____

20____ _____
_____
_____
_____
_____

20____ _____
_____
_____
_____
_____

20 ___ _____
_____
_____
_____
_____

20 ___ _____
_____
_____
_____
_____

20 ___ _____
_____
_____
_____
_____

20 ___ _____
_____
_____
_____
_____

20 ___ _____
_____
_____
_____
_____

20 _____ _____

20 _____ _____

20 _____ _____

20 _____ _____

20 _____ _____

20 _____ _____

20 _____ _____

20 _____ _____

20 _____ _____

20 _____ _____

APRIL 23

20 ___ _____

_____

_____

_____

_____

20 ___ _____

_____

_____

_____

_____

20 ___ _____

_____

_____

_____

_____

20 ___ _____

_____

_____

_____

_____

20 ___ _____

_____

_____

_____

_____

20 ___ _____
_____
_____
_____
_____

20 ___ _____
_____
_____
_____
_____

20 ___ _____
_____
_____
_____
_____

20 ___ _____
_____
_____
_____
_____

20 ___ _____
_____
_____
_____
_____

20 _____ _____
_____
_____
_____
_____
_____

20 _____ _____
_____
_____
_____
_____

20 _____ _____
_____
_____
_____
_____

20 _____ _____
_____
_____
_____
_____

20 _____ _____
_____
_____
_____
_____

APRIL 26

20 ___ _____

_____
_____
_____
_____

20 ___ _____

_____
_____
_____
_____

20 ___ _____

_____
_____
_____
_____

20 ___ _____

_____
_____
_____
_____

20 ___ _____

_____
_____
_____
_____

APRIL 27

20 _____

20 _____

20 _____

20 _____

20 _____

APRIL 28

20 ___ _____

20 ___ _____

20 ___ _____

20 ___ _____

20 ___ _____

20 ___ _____

20 ___ _____

20 ___ _____

20 ___ _____

20 ___ _____

APRIL 30

20 _____ _____

20 _____ _____

20 _____ _____

20 _____ _____

20 _____ _____

MAY 1

20 _____ _____

20 _____ _____

20 _____ _____

20 _____ _____

20 _____ _____

20 _____ _____
_____
_____
_____
_____

20 _____ _____
_____
_____
_____
_____

20 _____ _____
_____
_____
_____
_____

20 _____ _____
_____
_____
_____
_____

20 _____ _____
_____
_____
_____
_____

20 ___ _____
_____
_____
_____
_____

20 ___ _____
_____
_____
_____
_____

20 ___ _____
_____
_____
_____
_____

20 ___ _____
_____
_____
_____
_____

20 ___ _____
_____
_____
_____
_____

MAY 4

20 _____ _____

20 _____ _____

20 _____ _____

20 _____ _____

20 _____ _____

MAY 5

20 ___ _____
_____
_____
_____
_____

20 ___ _____
_____
_____
_____
_____

20 ___ _____
_____
_____
_____
_____

20 ___ _____
_____
_____
_____
_____

20 ___ _____
_____
_____
_____
_____

MAY 6

20___

20___

20___

20___

20___

MAY 7

20 ___ _____

20 ___ _____

20 ___ _____

20 ___ _____

20 ___ _____

20 ___ _____
_____
_____
_____
_____

20 ___ _____
_____
_____
_____
_____

20 ___ _____
_____
_____
_____
_____

20 ___ _____
_____
_____
_____
_____

20 ___ _____
_____
_____
_____
_____

20 ____ _____

20 ____ _____

20 ____ _____

20 ____ _____

20 ____ _____

20 ___ _____
_____
_____
_____
_____
_____

20 ___ _____
_____
_____
_____
_____
_____

20 ___ _____
_____
_____
_____
_____
_____

20 ___ _____
_____
_____
_____
_____
_____

20 ___ _____
_____
_____
_____
_____

MAY 11

20 _____

20 _____

20 _____

20 _____

20 _____

20 _____ _____

_____

_____

_____

_____

20 _____ _____

_____

_____

_____

_____

20 _____ _____

_____

_____

_____

_____

20 _____ _____

_____

_____

_____

_____

20 _____ _____

_____

_____

_____

_____

20 ____ _____
_____
_____
_____
_____

20 ____ _____
_____
_____
_____
_____

20 ____ _____
_____
_____
_____
_____

20 ____ _____
_____
_____
_____
_____

20 ____ _____
_____
_____
_____
_____

MAY 14

20 ___ _____

20 ___ _____

20 ___ _____

20 ___ _____

20 ___ _____

20 ___ _____

20 ___ _____

20 ___ _____

20 ___ _____

20 ___ _____

MAY 16

20____ _____

20____ _____

20____ _____

20____ _____

20____ _____

MAY 17

20 __ _____

20 __ _____

20 __ _____

20 __ _____

20 __ _____

20 ___ _____

_____

_____

_____

_____

20 ___ _____

_____

_____

_____

_____

20 ___ _____

_____

_____

_____

_____

20 ___ _____

_____

_____

_____

_____

20 ___ _____

_____

_____

_____

_____

20 _____

20 _____

20 _____

20 _____

20 _____

MAY 20

20 ___

_____

20 ___

_____

20 ___

_____

20 ___

_____

20 ___

_____

MAY 21

20 ___ _____

20 ___ _____

20 ___ _____

20 ___ _____

20 ___ _____

20 ___ _____
_____
_____
_____
_____

20 ___ _____
_____
_____
_____
_____

20 ___ _____
_____
_____
_____
_____

20 ___ _____
_____
_____
_____
_____

20 ___ _____
_____
_____
_____
_____

MAY 23

20 ___ _____

20 ___ _____

20 ___ _____

20 ___ _____

20 ___ _____

20 ___ _____
_____
_____
_____
_____

20 ___ _____
_____
_____
_____
_____

20 ___ _____
_____
_____
_____
_____

20 ___ _____
_____
_____
_____
_____

20 ___ _____
_____
_____
_____
_____

MAY 25

20 ___ _____

_____

_____

_____

_____

20 ___ _____

_____

_____

_____

_____

20 ___ _____

_____

_____

_____

_____

20 ___ _____

_____

_____

_____

_____

20 ___ _____

_____

_____

_____

_____

20 ___ _____

20 ___ _____

20 ___ _____

20 ___ _____

20 ___ _____

20 ___ _____
_____
_____
_____
_____

20 ___ _____
_____
_____
_____
_____

20 ___ _____
_____
_____
_____
_____

20 ___ _____
_____
_____
_____
_____

20 ___ _____
_____
_____
_____
_____

20 ___ _____

_____

_____

_____

_____

20 ___ _____

_____

_____

_____

_____

20 ___ _____

_____

_____

_____

_____

20 ___ _____

_____

_____

_____

_____

20 ___ _____

_____

_____

_____

_____

MAY 29

20 _____ _____

20 _____ _____

20 _____ _____

20 _____ _____

20 _____ _____

20 _____ _____

_____

_____

_____

_____

20 _____ _____

_____

_____

_____

_____

20 _____ _____

_____

_____

_____

_____

20 _____ _____

_____

_____

_____

_____

20 _____ _____

_____

_____

_____

_____

MAY 31

20 ___ _____

20 ___ _____

20 ___ _____

20 ___ _____

20 ___ _____

20 _____ _____
_____
_____
_____
_____

20 _____ _____
_____
_____
_____
_____

20 _____ _____
_____
_____
_____
_____

20 _____ _____
_____
_____
_____
_____

20 _____ _____
_____
_____
_____
_____

JUNE 2

20 _____ _____
_____
_____
_____
_____

20 _____ _____
_____
_____
_____
_____

20 _____ _____
_____
_____
_____
_____

20 _____ _____
_____
_____
_____
_____

20 _____ _____
_____
_____
_____
_____

JUNE 3

20 _____ _____

20 _____ _____

20 _____ _____

20 _____ _____

20 _____ _____

JUNE 4

20 ___ _____

20 ___ _____

20 ___ _____

20 ___ _____

20 ___ _____

20 _____ _____

20 _____ _____

20 _____ _____

20 _____ _____

20 _____ _____

20 ___ _____

20 ___ _____

20 ___ _____

20 ___ _____

20 ___ _____

20 _____ _____

20 _____ _____

20 _____ _____

20 _____ _____

20 _____ _____

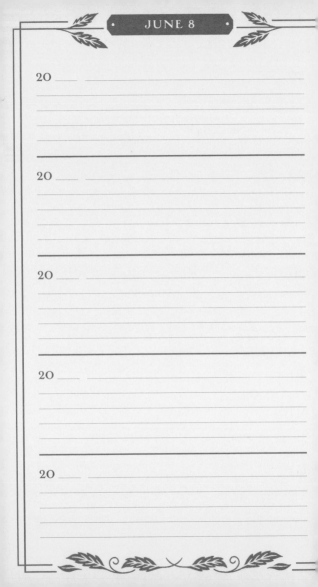

JUNE 8

20___

20___

20___

20___

20___

JUNE 9

20 ___ _____

20 ___ _____

20 ___ _____

20 ___ _____

20 ___ _____

20 ___

20 ___

20 ___

20 ___

20 ___

JUNE 11

20 _____ _____

20 _____ _____

20 _____ _____

20 _____ _____

20 _____ _____

JUNE 12

20___ _____

20___ _____

20___ _____

20___ _____

20___ _____

JUNE 13

20 ___ _____
_____
_____
_____
_____

20 ___ _____
_____
_____
_____
_____

20 ___ _____
_____
_____
_____
_____

20 ___ _____
_____
_____
_____
_____

20 ___ _____
_____
_____
_____
_____

20 _____ _____
_____
_____
_____
_____

20 _____ _____
_____
_____
_____
_____

20 _____ _____
_____
_____
_____
_____

20 _____ _____
_____
_____
_____
_____

20 _____ _____
_____
_____
_____
_____

JUNE 15

20 ___ _____

_____
_____
_____
_____

20 ___ _____

_____
_____
_____
_____

20 ___ _____

_____
_____
_____
_____

20 ___ _____

_____
_____
_____
_____

20 ___ _____

_____
_____
_____
_____

JUNE 16

20 _____ _____
_____
_____
_____
_____

20 _____ _____
_____
_____
_____
_____

20 _____ _____
_____
_____
_____
_____

20 _____ _____
_____
_____
_____
_____

20 _____ _____
_____
_____
_____
_____

20 ___ _____

_____

_____

_____

_____

20 ___ _____

_____

_____

_____

_____

20 ___ _____

_____

_____

_____

_____

20 ___ _____

_____

_____

_____

_____

20 ___ _____

_____

_____

_____

_____

20 ___ _____

20 ___ _____

20 ___ _____

20 ___ _____

20 ___ _____

JUNE 19

20 ___ _____
_____
_____
_____
_____

20 ___ _____
_____
_____
_____
_____

20 ___ _____
_____
_____
_____
_____

20 ___ _____
_____
_____
_____
_____

20 ___ _____
_____
_____
_____
_____

20 ___ _____
_____
_____
_____
_____

20 ___ _____
_____
_____
_____
_____

20 ___ _____
_____
_____
_____
_____

20 ___ _____
_____
_____
_____
_____

20 ___ _____
_____
_____
_____
_____

JUNE 21

20____

20____

20____

20____

20____

20___ _____

20___ _____

20___ _____

20___ _____

20___ _____

20 ___ _____
_____
_____
_____
_____

20 ___ _____
_____
_____
_____
_____

20 ___ _____
_____
_____
_____
_____

20 ___ _____
_____
_____
_____
_____

20 ___ _____
_____
_____
_____
_____

20 _____ _____

20 _____ _____

20 _____ _____

20 _____ _____

20 _____ _____

JUNE 25

20 ___ _____

_____

_____

_____

_____

20 ___ _____

_____

_____

_____

_____

20 ___ _____

_____

_____

_____

_____

20 ___ _____

_____

_____

_____

_____

20 ___ _____

_____

_____

_____

_____

20 _____ _____
_____
_____
_____
_____

20 _____ _____
_____
_____
_____
_____

20 _____ _____
_____
_____
_____
_____

20 _____ _____
_____
_____
_____
_____

20 _____ _____
_____
_____
_____
_____

20 ___ _____
_____
_____
_____
_____

20 ___ _____
_____
_____
_____
_____

20 ___ _____
_____
_____
_____
_____

20 ___ _____
_____
_____
_____
_____

20 ___ _____
_____
_____
_____
_____

20 _____ _____

20 _____ _____

20 _____ _____

20 _____ _____

20 _____ _____

JUNE 29

20 _____ _____

20 _____ _____

20 _____ _____

20 _____ _____

20 _____ _____

JUNE 30

20 ___ _____
_____
_____
_____
_____

20 ___ _____
_____
_____
_____
_____

20 ___ _____
_____
_____
_____
_____

20 ___ _____
_____
_____
_____
_____

20 ___ _____
_____
_____
_____
_____

20 _____ _____

20 _____ _____

20 _____ _____

20 _____ _____

20 _____ _____

20 _____ _____

20 _____ _____

20 _____ _____

20 _____ _____

20 _____ _____

20 _____

20 _____

20 _____

20 _____

20 _____

JULY 4

20 ___ _____
_____
_____
_____
_____

20 ___ _____
_____
_____
_____
_____

20 ___ _____
_____
_____
_____
_____

20 ___ _____
_____
_____
_____
_____

20 ___ _____
_____
_____
_____
_____

20 _____ _____

20 _____ _____

20 _____ _____

20 _____ _____

20 _____ _____

JULY 6

20 _____

20 _____

20 _____

20 _____

20 _____

20 ___ _____
_____
_____
_____
_____

20 ___ _____
_____
_____
_____
_____

20 ___ _____
_____
_____
_____
_____

20 ___ _____
_____
_____
_____
_____

20 ___ _____
_____
_____
_____
_____

JULY 8

20 ___ _____

20 ___ _____

20 ___ _____

20 ___ _____

20 ___ _____

JULY 9

20 ___ _____

20 ___ _____

20 ___ _____

20 ___ _____

20 ___ _____

20 ___ _____

20 ___ _____

20 ___ _____

20 ___ _____

20 ___ _____

JULY 11

20 ___ _____

20 ___ _____

20 ___ _____

20 ___ _____

20 ___ _____

20 ___ _____
_____
_____
_____
_____
_____

20 ___ _____
_____
_____
_____
_____
_____

20 ___ _____
_____
_____
_____
_____
_____

20 ___ _____
_____
_____
_____
_____
_____

20 ___ _____
_____
_____
_____
_____

JULY 13

20 ___ _____

20 ___ _____

20 ___ _____

20 ___ _____

20 ___ _____

JULY 14

20___ _____

20___ _____

20___ _____

20___ _____

20___ _____

20 ___ _____

_____

_____

_____

_____

20 ___ _____

_____

_____

_____

_____

20 ___ _____

_____

_____

_____

_____

20 ___ _____

_____

_____

_____

_____

20 ___ _____

_____

_____

_____

_____

20 ___ _____

_____

_____

_____

_____

20 ___ _____

_____

_____

_____

20 ___ _____

_____

_____

_____

20 ___ _____

_____

_____

_____

20 ___ _____

_____

_____

_____

JULY 17

20 ___ _____

20 ___ _____

20 ___ _____

20 ___ _____

20 ___ _____

20____

20____

20____

20____

20____

20 ___

20 ___

20 ___

20 ___

20 ___

20 ___ _____

_____

_____

_____

_____

20 ___ _____

_____

_____

_____

_____

20 ___ _____

_____

_____

_____

_____

20 ___ _____

_____

_____

_____

_____

20 ___ _____

_____

_____

_____

_____

20 _____ _____
_____
_____
_____
_____

20 _____ _____
_____
_____
_____
_____

20 _____ _____
_____
_____
_____
_____

20 _____ _____
_____
_____
_____
_____

20 _____ _____
_____
_____
_____
_____

JULY 22

20 ___

20 ___

20 ___

20 ___

20 ___

20 ___ _____

20 ___ _____

20 ___ _____

20 ___ _____

20 ___ _____

JULY 24

20 _____ _____

_____

_____

_____

_____

20 _____ _____

_____

_____

_____

_____

20 _____ _____

_____

_____

_____

_____

20 _____ _____

_____

_____

_____

_____

20 _____ _____

_____

_____

_____

_____

20 ___

_____

_____

_____

_____

20 ___

_____

_____

_____

_____

20 ___

_____

_____

_____

_____

20 ___

_____

_____

_____

_____

20 ___

_____

_____

_____

_____

20 ___ _____
_____
_____
_____
_____
_____

20 ___ _____
_____
_____
_____
_____
_____

20 ___ _____
_____
_____
_____
_____
_____

20 ___ _____
_____
_____
_____
_____
_____

20 ___ _____
_____
_____
_____
_____

JULY 27

20

20

20

20

20

JULY 28

20 ___

20 ___

20 ___

20 ___

20 ___

20 _____ _____

_____

_____

_____

_____

20 _____ _____

_____

_____

_____

_____

20 _____ _____

_____

_____

_____

_____

20 _____ _____

_____

_____

_____

_____

20 _____ _____

_____

_____

_____

_____

20 ___ _____
_____
_____
_____
_____

20 ___ _____
_____
_____
_____
_____

20 ___ _____
_____
_____
_____
_____

20 ___ _____
_____
_____
_____
_____

20 ___ _____
_____
_____
_____
_____

20 ___ _____

20 ___ _____

20 ___ _____

20 ___ _____

20 ___ _____

20 _____ _____
_____
_____
_____
_____

20 _____ _____
_____
_____
_____
_____

20 _____ _____
_____
_____
_____
_____

20 _____ _____
_____
_____
_____
_____

20 _____ _____
_____
_____
_____
_____

20 ___ _____

_____

_____

_____

_____

20 ___ _____

_____

_____

_____

_____

20 ___ _____

_____

_____

_____

_____

20 ___ _____

_____

_____

_____

_____

20 ___ _____

_____

_____

_____

_____

AUGUST 3

20 ___

20 ___

20 ___

20 ___

20 ___

AUGUST 4

20 ___ _____

_____

_____

_____

_____

20 ___ _____

_____

_____

_____

_____

20 ___ _____

_____

_____

_____

_____

20 ___ _____

_____

_____

_____

_____

20 ___ _____

_____

_____

_____

_____

20 _____ _____

_____

_____

_____

_____

_____

20 _____ _____

_____

_____

_____

_____

_____

20 _____ _____

_____

_____

_____

_____

_____

20 _____ _____

_____

_____

_____

_____

_____

20 _____ _____

_____

_____

_____

_____

_____

AUGUST 6

20 ___ _____
_____
_____
_____
_____

20 ___ _____
_____
_____
_____
_____

20 ___ _____
_____
_____
_____
_____

20 ___ _____
_____
_____
_____
_____

20 ___ _____
_____
_____
_____
_____

20 ___ _____
_____
_____
_____
_____
_____

20 ___ _____
_____
_____
_____
_____
_____

20 ___ _____
_____
_____
_____
_____
_____

20 ___ _____
_____
_____
_____
_____
_____

20 ___ _____
_____
_____
_____
_____
_____

20 _____ _____

20 _____ _____

20 _____ _____

20 _____ _____

20 _____ _____

20 ___ _____

20 ___ _____

20 ___ _____

20 ___ _____

20 ___ _____

20 ___ _____
_____
_____
_____
_____

20 ___ _____
_____
_____
_____
_____

20 ___ _____
_____
_____
_____
_____

20 ___ _____
_____
_____
_____
_____

20 ___ _____
_____
_____
_____
_____

20 ___ _____

20 ___ _____

20 ___ _____

20 ___ _____

20 ___ _____

AUGUST 12

20 ___ _____

20 ___ _____

20 ___ _____

20 ___ _____

20 ___ _____

20 _____ _____

20 _____ _____

20 _____ _____

20 _____ _____

20 _____ _____

20 ___ _____

20 ___ _____

20 ___ _____

20 ___ _____

20 ___ _____

20 ___ _____

20 ___ _____

20 ___ _____

20 ___ _____

20 ___ _____

AUGUST 16

20 ___ _____

_____

_____

_____

_____

20 ___ _____

_____

_____

_____

_____

20 ___ _____

_____

_____

_____

_____

20 ___ _____

_____

_____

_____

_____

20 ___ _____

_____

_____

_____

_____

20 _____ _____
_____
_____
_____
_____

20 _____ _____
_____
_____
_____
_____

20 _____ _____
_____
_____
_____
_____

20 _____ _____
_____
_____
_____
_____

20 _____ _____
_____
_____
_____
_____

20 _____ _____

20 _____ _____

20 _____ _____

20 _____ _____

20 _____ _____

20 _____ _____
_____
_____
_____
_____

20 _____ _____
_____
_____
_____
_____

20 _____ _____
_____
_____
_____
_____

20 _____ _____
_____
_____
_____
_____

20 _____ _____
_____
_____
_____
_____

20 ___ _____

_____

_____

_____

_____

20 ___ _____

_____

_____

_____

_____

20 ___ _____

_____

_____

_____

_____

20 ___ _____

_____

_____

_____

_____

20 ___ _____

_____

_____

_____

_____

AUGUST 21

20____ _____

20____ _____

20____ _____

20____ _____

20____ _____

20 _____ _____
_____
_____
_____
_____
_____

20 _____ _____
_____
_____
_____
_____
_____

20 _____ _____
_____
_____
_____
_____
_____

20 _____ _____
_____
_____
_____
_____
_____

20 _____ _____
_____
_____
_____
_____
_____

AUGUST 23

20 ___ _____

20 ___ _____

20 ___ _____

20 ___ _____

20 ___ _____

20 _____ _____

20 _____ _____

20 _____ _____

20 _____ _____

20 _____ _____

20 ___ _____

20 ___ _____

20 ___ _____

20 ___ _____

20 ___ _____

20 ___ _____

_____

_____

_____

_____

20 ___ _____

_____

_____

_____

_____

20 ___ _____

_____

_____

_____

_____

20 ___ _____

_____

_____

_____

_____

20 ___ _____

_____

_____

_____

_____

20 ___ _____

_____

_____

_____

_____

20 ___ _____

_____

_____

_____

_____

20 ___ _____

_____

_____

_____

_____

20 ___ _____

_____

_____

_____

_____

20 ___ _____

_____

_____

_____

_____

AUGUST 28

20 ___ _____

20 ___ _____

20 ___ _____

20 ___ _____

20 ___ _____

AUGUST 29

20___ _____

20___ _____

20___ _____

20___ _____

20___ _____

AUGUST 30

20 _____ _____

20 _____ _____

20 _____ _____

20 _____ _____

20 _____ _____

20___ _____

_____

_____

_____

_____

20___ _____

_____

_____

_____

_____

20___ _____

_____

_____

_____

_____

20___ _____

_____

_____

_____

_____

20___ _____

_____

_____

_____

_____

20 _____ _____

20 _____ _____

20 _____ _____

20 _____ _____

20 _____ _____

20 ___ _____

20 ___ _____

20 ___ _____

20 ___ _____

20 ___ _____

SEPTEMBER 3

20 _____ _____

20 _____ _____

20 _____ _____

20 _____ _____

20 _____ _____

20 _____ _____

20 _____ _____

20 _____ _____

20 _____ _____

20 _____ _____

20 ___

20 ___

20 ___

20 ___

20 ___

20 ___

20 ___

20 ___

20 ___

20 ___

SEPTEMBER 7

20____ _____

20____ _____

20____ _____

20____ _____

20____ _____

20 ___ _____

20 ___ _____

20 ___ _____

20 ___ _____

20 ___ _____

SEPTEMBER 9

20 ___ _____

20 ___ _____

20 ___ _____

20 ___ _____

20 ___ _____

20 _____ _____
_____
_____
_____
_____
_____

20 _____ _____
_____
_____
_____
_____
_____

20 _____ _____
_____
_____
_____
_____
_____

20 _____ _____
_____
_____
_____
_____
_____

20 _____ _____
_____
_____
_____
_____

· SEPTEMBER 11 ·

20 ___ _____

20 ___ _____

20 ___ _____

20 ___ _____

20 ___ _____

20 ___ _____

20 ___ _____

20 ___ _____

20 ___ _____

20 ___ _____

20 _____

20 _____

20 _____

20 _____

20 _____

20 ___ _____

20 ___ _____

20 ___ _____

20 ___ _____

20 ___ _____

20 ___ _____

20 ___ _____

20 ___ _____

20 ___ _____

20 ___ _____

20 —— ——————————————

20 —— ——————————————

20 —— ——————————————

20 —— ——————————————

20 —— ——————————————

· SEPTEMBER 17 ·

20 ___ _____

_____

_____

_____

_____

20 ___ _____

_____

_____

_____

_____

20 ___ _____

_____

_____

_____

_____

20 ___ _____

_____

_____

_____

_____

20 ___ _____

_____

_____

_____

_____

20 ___ _____
_____
_____
_____
_____

20 ___ _____
_____
_____
_____
_____

20 ___ _____
_____
_____
_____
_____

20 ___ _____
_____
_____
_____
_____

20 ___ _____
_____
_____
_____
_____

20 ___

20 ___

20 ___

20 ___

20 ___

20 ___ _____

20 ___ _____

20 ___ _____

20 ___ _____

20 ___ _____

20 ___ _____

20 ___ _____

20 ___ _____

20 ___ _____

20 ___ _____

· SEPTEMBER 22 ·

20 ___ _____

20 ___ _____

20 ___ _____

20 ___ _____

20 ___ _____

20 ___ _____
_____
_____
_____
_____

20 ___ _____
_____
_____
_____
_____

20 ___ _____
_____
_____
_____
_____

20 ___ _____
_____
_____
_____
_____

20 ___ _____
_____
_____
_____
_____

20 _____ _____
_____
_____
_____
_____

20 _____ _____
_____
_____
_____
_____

20 _____ _____
_____
_____
_____
_____

20 _____ _____
_____
_____
_____
_____

20 _____ _____
_____
_____
_____
_____

20 ___ _____
_____
_____
_____
_____

20 ___ _____
_____
_____
_____
_____

20 ___ _____
_____
_____
_____
_____

20 ___ _____
_____
_____
_____
_____

20 ___ _____
_____
_____
_____
_____

20 _____ _____

20 _____ _____

20 _____ _____

20 _____ _____

20 _____ _____

20 _____ _____

_____

_____

_____

_____

20 _____ _____

_____

_____

_____

_____

20 _____ _____

_____

_____

_____

_____

20 _____ _____

_____

_____

_____

_____

20 _____ _____

_____

_____

_____

_____

20 ___ _____
_____
_____
_____
_____

20 ___ _____
_____
_____
_____
_____

20 ___ _____
_____
_____
_____
_____

20 ___ _____
_____
_____
_____
_____

20 ___ _____
_____
_____
_____
_____

20 _____ _____
_____
_____
_____
_____

20 _____ _____
_____
_____
_____
_____

20 _____ _____
_____
_____
_____
_____

20 _____ _____
_____
_____
_____
_____

20 _____ _____
_____
_____
_____
_____

· SEPTEMBER 30 ·

20 _____ _____

20 _____ _____

20 _____ _____

20 _____ _____

20 _____ _____

20 _____ _____
_____
_____
_____
_____

20 _____ _____
_____
_____
_____
_____

20 _____ _____
_____
_____
_____
_____

20 _____ _____
_____
_____
_____
_____

20 _____ _____
_____
_____
_____
_____

20 ___ _____

20 ___ _____

20 ___ _____

20 ___ _____

20 ___ _____

OCTOBER 3

20 ___ _____

20 ___ _____

20 ___ _____

20 ___ _____

20 ___ _____

20 _____ _____
_____
_____
_____
_____

20 _____ _____
_____
_____
_____
_____

20 _____ _____
_____
_____
_____
_____

20 _____ _____
_____
_____
_____
_____

20 _____ _____
_____
_____
_____
_____

20 ___ _____

20 ___ _____

20 ___ _____

20 ___ _____

20 ___ _____

OCTOBER 6

20 ___ _____

20 ___ _____

20 ___ _____

20 ___ _____

20 ___ _____

OCTOBER 7

20 ___ _____

_____

_____

_____

_____

20 ___ _____

_____

_____

_____

_____

20 ___ _____

_____

_____

_____

_____

20 ___ _____

_____

_____

_____

_____

20 ___ _____

_____

_____

_____

_____

OCTOBER 8

20 ___ _____

20 ___ _____

20 ___ _____

20 ___ _____

20 ___ _____

20 _____ _____
_____
_____
_____
_____

20 _____ _____
_____
_____
_____
_____

20 _____ _____
_____
_____
_____
_____

20 _____ _____
_____
_____
_____
_____

20 _____ _____
_____
_____
_____
_____

20 ___ _____

20 ___ _____

20 ___ _____

20 ___ _____

20 ___ _____

20 ___ _____

20 ___ _____

20 ___ _____

20 ___ _____

20 ___ _____

20 _____ _____
_____
_____
_____
_____

20 _____ _____
_____
_____
_____
_____

20 _____ _____
_____
_____
_____
_____

20 _____ _____
_____
_____
_____
_____

20 _____ _____
_____
_____
_____
_____

20 _____ _____
_____
_____
_____
_____

20 _____ _____
_____
_____
_____
_____

20 _____ _____
_____
_____
_____
_____

20 _____ _____
_____
_____
_____
_____

20 _____ _____
_____
_____
_____
_____

20 ___ _____

_____

_____

_____

_____

20 ___ _____

_____

_____

_____

_____

20 ___ _____

_____

_____

_____

_____

20 ___ _____

_____

_____

_____

_____

20 ___ _____

_____

_____

_____

_____

20 _____ _____

20 _____ _____

20 _____ _____

20 _____ _____

20 _____ _____

20 ___ _____
_____
_____
_____
_____

20 ___ _____
_____
_____
_____
_____

20 ___ _____
_____
_____
_____
_____

20 ___ _____
_____
_____
_____
_____

20 ___ _____
_____
_____
_____
_____

20 ___ _____

_____

_____

_____

_____

20 ___ _____

_____

_____

_____

_____

20 ___ _____

_____

_____

_____

_____

20 ___ _____

_____

_____

_____

_____

20 ___ _____

_____

_____

_____

_____

20 ___ _____

_____

_____

_____

_____

20 ___ _____

_____

_____

_____

_____

20 ___ _____

_____

_____

_____

_____

20 ___ _____

_____

_____

_____

_____

20 ___ _____

_____

_____

_____

_____

20 ___ _____

_____

_____

_____

_____

20 ___ _____

_____

_____

_____

_____

20 ___ _____

_____

_____

_____

_____

20 ___ _____

_____

_____

_____

_____

20 ___ _____

_____

_____

_____

_____

20 ___ _____

_____

_____

_____

_____

20 ___ _____

_____

_____

_____

_____

20 ___ _____

_____

_____

_____

_____

20 ___ _____

_____

_____

_____

_____

20 ___ _____

_____

_____

_____

_____

20 ___ _____

20 ___ _____

20 ___ _____

20 ___ _____

20 ___ _____

20 ___ _____

20 ___ _____

20 ___ _____

20 ___ _____

20 ___ _____

· OCTOBER 23 ·

20 _____

20 _____

20 _____

20 _____

20 _____

20 ___ _____
_____
_____
_____
_____

20 ___ _____
_____
_____
_____
_____

20 ___ _____
_____
_____
_____

20 ___ _____
_____
_____
_____
_____

20 ___ _____
_____
_____
_____
_____

20 ___ _____

20 ___ _____

20 ___ _____

20 ___ _____

20 ___ _____

20 ___ _____

20 ___ _____

20 ___ _____

20 ___ _____

20 ___ _____

20 ___ _____
_____
_____
_____
_____

20 ___ _____
_____
_____
_____
_____

20 ___ _____
_____
_____
_____
_____

20 ___ _____
_____
_____
_____
_____
_____

20 ___ _____
_____
_____
_____
_____

20 ___ _____

20 ___ _____

20 ___ _____

20 ___ _____

20 ___ _____

20 ___ _____

20 ___ _____

20 ___ _____

20 ___ _____

20 ___ _____

20 ___ _____
_____
_____
_____
_____

20 ___ _____
_____
_____
_____
_____

20 ___ _____
_____
_____
_____
_____

20 ___ _____
_____
_____
_____
_____

20 ___ _____
_____
_____
_____
_____

OCTOBER 31

20 ___ _____

20 ___ _____

20 ___ _____

20 ___ _____

20 ___ _____

20____ _____
_____
_____
_____
_____

20____ _____
_____
_____
_____
_____

20____ _____
_____
_____
_____
_____

20____ _____
_____
_____
_____
_____

20____ _____
_____
_____
_____
_____

20 _____ _____
_____
_____
_____
_____

20 _____ _____
_____
_____
_____
_____

20 _____ _____
_____
_____
_____
_____

20 _____ _____
_____
_____
_____
_____

20 _____ _____
_____
_____
_____
_____

· NOVEMBER 3 ·

20___

20___

20___

20___

20___

20 _____ _____

20 _____ _____

20 _____ _____

20 _____ _____

20 _____ _____

20 ___ _____

20 ___ _____

20 ___ _____

20 ___ _____

20 ___ _____

20 ___ _____

20 ___ _____

20 ___ _____

20 ___ _____

20 ___ _____

20 ___ _____

_____

_____

_____

_____

_____

20 ___ _____

_____

_____

_____

_____

_____

20 ___ _____

_____

_____

_____

_____

_____

20 ___ _____

_____

_____

_____

_____

_____

20 ___ _____

_____

_____

_____

_____

_____

NOVEMBER 8

20 _____ _____

20 _____ _____

20 _____ _____

20 _____ _____

20 _____ _____

20 _____ _____

20 _____ _____

20 _____ _____

20 _____ _____

20 _____ _____

20____ _____

20____ _____

20____ _____

20____ _____

20____ _____

20 ___ _____

_____

_____

_____

_____

20 ___ _____

_____

_____

_____

_____

20 ___ _____

_____

_____

_____

_____

20 ___ _____

_____

_____

_____

_____

20 ___ _____

_____

_____

_____

_____

20 ____ _____

_____
_____
_____
_____
_____

20 ____ _____

_____
_____
_____
_____
_____

20 ____ _____

_____
_____
_____
_____
_____

20 ____ _____

_____
_____
_____
_____
_____

20 ____ _____

_____
_____
_____
_____
_____

· NOVEMBER 13 ·

20 ___ _____

20 ___ _____

20 ___ _____

20 ___ _____

20 ___ _____

20 ___ _____

_____

_____

_____

_____

20 ___ _____

_____

_____

_____

_____

20 ___ _____

_____

_____

_____

_____

20 ___ _____

_____

_____

_____

_____

20 ___ _____

_____

_____

_____

_____

20 ___ _____
_____
_____
_____
_____

20 ___ _____
_____
_____
_____
_____

20 ___ _____
_____
_____
_____
_____

20 ___ _____
_____
_____
_____
_____

20 ___ _____
_____
_____
_____
_____

20 ___ _____

20 ___ _____

20 ___ _____

20 ___ _____

20 ___ _____

20 ___ _____

20 ___ _____

20 ___ _____

20 ___ _____

20 ___ _____

20 ___ _____

20 ___ _____

20 ___ _____

20 ___ _____

20 ___ _____

20 ___ _____

_____

_____

_____

_____

20 ___ _____

_____

_____

_____

_____

20 ___ _____

_____

_____

_____

_____

20 ___ _____

_____

_____

_____

_____

20 ___ _____

_____

_____

_____

_____

20 ___ _____

20 ___ _____

20 ___ _____

20 ___ _____

20 ___ _____

20 _____ _____

_____

_____

_____

_____

20 _____ _____

_____

_____

_____

_____

20 _____ _____

_____

_____

_____

_____

20 _____ _____

_____

_____

_____

_____

20 _____ _____

_____

_____

_____

_____

• NOVEMBER 22 •

20 _____

20 _____

20 _____

20 _____

20 _____

20 ___

20 ___

20 ___

20 ___

20 ___

· NOVEMBER 24 ·

20 _____ _____

20 _____ _____

20 _____ _____

20 _____ _____

20 _____ _____

20 ___ _____

20 ___ _____

20 ___ _____

20 ___ _____

20 ___ _____

· NOVEMBER 26 ·

20 ___

_____
_____
_____
_____
_____

20 ___

_____
_____
_____
_____
_____

20 ___

_____
_____
_____
_____
_____

20 ___

_____
_____
_____
_____
_____

20 ___

_____
_____
_____
_____
_____

20 ___ _____

20 ___ _____

20 ___ _____

20 ___ _____

20 ___ _____

20 ___ _____

_____

_____

_____

_____

20 ___ _____

_____

_____

_____

_____

20 ___ _____

_____

_____

_____

_____

20 ___ _____

_____

_____

_____

_____

20 ___ _____

_____

_____

_____

_____

20 _____ _____

20 _____ _____

20 _____ _____

20 _____ _____

20 _____ _____

20 ___

20 ___

20 ___

20 ___

20 ___

20 ___ _____

_____

_____

_____

_____

20 ___ _____

_____

_____

_____

_____

20 ___ _____

_____

_____

_____

_____

20 ___ _____

_____

_____

_____

_____

20 ___ _____

_____

_____

_____

_____

20 ___ _____

_____

_____

_____

_____

20 ___ _____

_____

_____

_____

_____

20 ___ _____

_____

_____

_____

_____

20 ___ _____

_____

_____

_____

_____

20 ___ _____

_____

_____

_____

_____

20 ___ _____

20 ___ _____

20 ___ _____

20 ___ _____

20 ___ _____

20 ___ _____

20 ___ _____

20 ___ _____

20 ___ _____

20 ___ _____

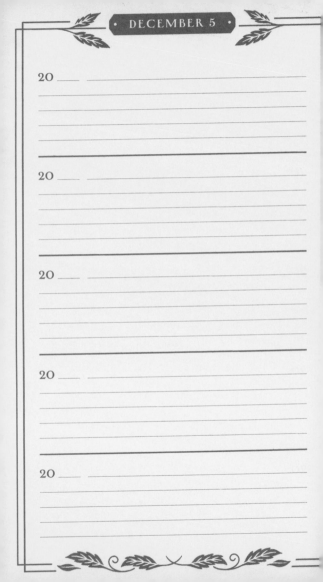

DECEMBER 5

20 ____ _____
_____
_____
_____
_____
_____

20 ____ _____
_____
_____
_____
_____
_____

20 ____ _____
_____
_____
_____
_____
_____

20 ____ _____
_____
_____
_____
_____
_____

20 ____ _____
_____
_____
_____
_____
_____

20 ___ _____

_____

_____

_____

_____

20 ___ _____

_____

_____

_____

_____

20 ___ _____

_____

_____

_____

_____

20 ___ _____

_____

_____

_____

_____

20 ___ _____

_____

_____

_____

_____

DECEMBER 7

20 ___ _____

_____
_____
_____
_____

20 ___ _____

_____
_____
_____
_____

20 ___ _____

_____
_____
_____
_____

20 ___ _____

_____
_____
_____
_____

20 ___ _____

_____
_____
_____
_____

DECEMBER 8

20 ___ _____

20 ___ _____

20 ___ _____

20 ___ _____

20 ___ _____

DECEMBER 9

20 ___ _____

20 ___ _____

20 ___ _____

20 ___ _____

20 ___ _____

20 __ _____
_____
_____
_____
_____

20 __ _____
_____
_____
_____
_____

20 __ _____
_____
_____
_____
_____

20 __ _____
_____
_____
_____
_____

20 __ _____
_____
_____
_____
_____

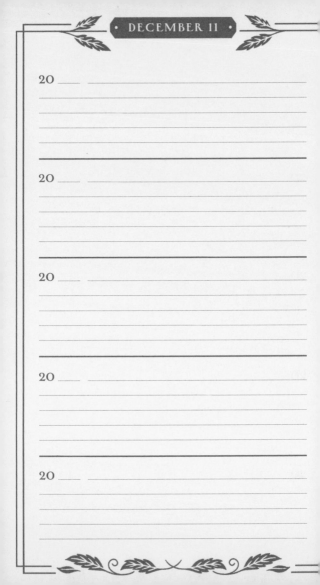

· DECEMBER 11 ·

20 ___ _____

_____

_____

_____

_____

20 ___ _____

_____

_____

_____

_____

20 ___ _____

_____

_____

_____

_____

20 ___ _____

_____

_____

_____

_____

20 ___ _____

_____

_____

_____

_____

20 ___ _____

20 ___ _____

20 ___ _____

20 ___ _____

20 ___ _____

20 ___ _____

20 ___ _____

20 ___ _____

20 ___ _____

20 ___ _____

DECEMBER 14

20 _____

20 _____

20 _____

20 _____

20 _____

20 ___ _____

_____

_____

_____

_____

20 ___ _____

_____

_____

_____

_____

20 ___ _____

_____

_____

_____

_____

20 ___ _____

_____

_____

_____

_____

20 ___ _____

_____

_____

_____

_____

20 _____ _____

20 _____ _____

20 _____ _____

20 _____ _____

20 _____ _____

20 _____ _____

_____

_____

_____

_____

20 _____ _____

_____

_____

_____

_____

20 _____ _____

_____

_____

_____

_____

20 _____ _____

_____

_____

_____

_____

20 _____ _____

_____

_____

_____

_____

20 _____ _____

20 _____ _____

20 _____ _____

20 _____ _____

20 _____ _____

· DECEMBER 23 ·

20____

20____

20____

20____

20____

20 ___ _____

20 ___ _____

20 ___ _____

20 ___ _____

20 ___ _____

• DECEMBER 25 •

20 ___ _____
_____
_____
_____
_____
_____

20 ___ _____
_____
_____
_____
_____
_____

20 ___ _____
_____
_____
_____
_____

20 ___ _____
_____
_____
_____
_____
_____

20 ___ _____
_____
_____
_____
_____

20 _____ _____

20 _____ _____

20 _____ _____

20 _____ _____

20 _____ _____

· DECEMBER 27 ·

20___ _____

20___ _____

20___ _____

20___ _____

20___ _____

20 ___ _____

20 ___ _____

20 ___ _____

20 ___ _____

20 ___ _____

20 __ _____

20 __ _____

20 __ _____

20 __ _____

20 __ _____

20 ___ _____

20 ___ _____

20 ___ _____

20 ___ _____

20 ___ _____

20 _____ _____
_____
_____
_____
_____

20 _____ _____
_____
_____
_____
_____

20 _____ _____
_____
_____
_____
_____

20 _____ _____
_____
_____
_____
_____

20 _____ _____
_____
_____
_____
_____

DATES TO REMEMBER

DATES TO REMEMBER

_____
_____
_____
_____
_____
_____
_____
_____
_____
_____
_____
_____
_____
_____
_____
_____
_____
_____
_____
_____
_____
_____
_____
_____
_____
_____